Reparation To The Sacred And Immaculate Heart

A Journey of Devotion, Adoration, Prayers, Meditations and Reflections

Alice Davidson

Copyright © 2024 by
(Alice Davidson)

All rights reserved. All writings are inspired by the Holy Spirit.

No part of this publication may be reproduced, distributed, or transmitted in any form or by any means, including photocopying, recording, or other electronic or mechanical methods, without the prior written permission of the publisher, except in the case of brief quotations embodied in critical reviews and certain other noncommercial uses permitted by copyright law.

TABLE OF CONTENT

SECTION ONE..7
INTRODUCTION TO THE PRAYER......................7
SECTION TWO..13
SIGNIFICANCE OF THIS PRAYER.................... 13
SECTION THREE..17
PRAYING REPARATION PRAYERS
EFFECTIVELY...17
SECTION FOUR..25
Prayers Of Contrition..25
Effective prayer for contrition, expressing a sincere plea for God's mercy and forgiveness:...................31
SECTION FIVE..36
Litany of the Sacred Heart................................ 36
SECTION SIX..44
Sorrowful Mysteries Of The Rosary With A
Focus On Reparation..44
SECTION SEVEN..49
Prayer of Devotion to the Sacred Heart............49
Holy hour of Reparation Prayer, Reflection and meditation to the Sacred Heart of Jesus...............54
SECTION EIGHT... 69
Prayer of Reparation to the Immaculate Heart of
Mary..69
SECTION NINE...83
Additional prayers of reparation to the Sacred
Heart of Jesus.. 83
SECTION TEN..91

Additional reparation prayers to the Immaculate Heart of Mary... 91
CONCLUSION... 99

THANK YOU FOR FINDING THIS BOOK WORTHY AS YOU EMBARK ON THIS JOURNEY OF REPARATION MAY YOU RECEIVE THE TOUCH OF THE HOLY SPIRIT, MERCY, GRACE, FAVOR, DIVINE GUIDANCE AND DIRECTION THROUGH THE PRAYERS, REFLECTIONS AND MEDITATIONS IN THE NAME OF THE FATHER THE SON AND THE HOLY SPIRIT

SECTION ONE

INTRODUCTION TO THE PRAYER

Reparation prayers hold profound significance within the Catholic tradition, embodying the spirit of contrition, love, and a desire for healing and restoration.

Here are key points highlighting the importance of reparation prayers:

1. Acknowledgment of Sin:

Reparation prayers begin with a sincere acknowledgment of personal and collective sin. This humility recognizes the need for forgiveness and reconciliation with God, emphasizing the importance of contrition as a starting point for spiritual growth.

2. Expression of Love and Gratitude: These prayers are not solely focused on seeking forgiveness; they also express profound love and gratitude for the mercy and compassion of God. Reparation prayers demonstrate a heartfelt desire to repair the relationship with the divine and to reciprocate God's boundless love.

3. Alignment with Christian Virtues:
Reparation prayers often emphasize virtues such as humility, repentance, and a commitment to living a more virtuous life. By aligning with these Christian values, individuals actively seek to transform their lives in accordance with the teachings of Christ.

4. Participation in Christ's Redemptive Work:
The concept of offering prayers of reparation aligns with the belief that believers can participate in Christ's redemptive work. By acknowledging and atoning for sin, individuals see

themselves as contributing to the ongoing process of redemption and reconciliation initiated by Christ's sacrifice on the Cross.

5. A Path to Healing and Wholeness: Reparation prayers provide a path to healing and wholeness, both individually and collectively. Through the act of repentance and seeking forgiveness, individuals open themselves to the transformative power of God's grace, experiencing a renewal of spirit and a restoration of the soul.

6. Promotion of Social Justice:
Reparation prayers extend beyond personal repentance to address social injustices. This aspect is particularly relevant in the context of recognizing and atoning for societal sins, fostering a commitment to social justice and solidarity with those who are marginalized or oppressed.

7. Restoration of Relationship with God:
At its core, reparation prayers aim to restore the intimate relationship between individuals and God. Through genuine contrition, believers seek to mend the bonds that

may have been strained by sin, reestablishing a connection characterized by love, trust, and communion.

Reparation prayers hold significant meaning in the Catholic faith as a means of acknowledging sin, expressing love and gratitude, aligning with Christian virtues, participating in Christ's redemptive work, fostering healing, addressing social injustices, and ultimately seeking the restoration of a deep and meaningful relationship with God.

SECTION TWO

SIGNIFICANCE OF THIS PRAYER

The Act of Reparation to the Sacred Heart is a powerful and meaningful prayer within the Catholic tradition, expressing profound love, contrition, and a desire for spiritual renewal.

Central to the Act of Reparation is a sincere expression of contrition for personal and collective sins. This acknowledgment of wrongdoing is an essential step toward seeking reconciliation with God and embracing the transformative power of repentance. The prayer expresses a desire to make amends for the offenses committed against the Sacred Heart. By offering acts of reparation, individuals express a genuine commitment to rectify the wounds caused by sin and to contribute to the healing process initiated by Christ's sacrifice.

It serves as a solemn pledge of devotion to the Sacred Heart. It signifies a commitment to living a life aligned with Christian virtues, guided by the love and teachings of Jesus, and actively participating in the redemptive work of Christ.A significant aspect of the prayer involves the voluntary offering of oneself to the Sacred Heart. This act symbolizes a surrender of one's will, desires, and shortcomings to Christ, inviting His transformative grace into every aspect of life.It acknowledges human frailty and imperfection while relying on the boundless mercy of the Sacred Heart to cleanse and purify the soul.

By engaging in the Act of Reparation, individuals actively participate in their own spiritual renewal. The prayer becomes a catalyst for personal growth, deepening the connection with the Sacred Heart and fostering a more profound understanding of God's love and mercy.

The Act of Reparation to the Sacred Heart is a heartfelt and transformative prayer that combines contrition, devotion, and a commitment to live in accordance with the teachings of Christ. It serves as a powerful means of seeking reconciliation, expressing love, and actively participating in the ongoing process of redemption through the Sacred Heart of Jesus.

SECTION THREE

PRAYING REPARATION PRAYERS EFFECTIVELY

Praying reparation prayers effectively involves engaging with sincerity, reverence, and a genuine desire for spiritual growth and reconciliation. It involved some sacred approaches which are:

1. Begin with a Humble Heart:
Approach your prayer with humility, acknowledging your need for God's mercy and forgiveness. Recognize the

gravity of sin and the desire for healing and renewal in your life.

2. Create a Sacred Space:
Find a quiet and peaceful place free from distractions. Create a sacred space where you can focus on your prayers without interruptions, allowing for a deeper connection with God.

3. Center Yourself in Silence:
Begin your prayer time with a few moments of silence. Center yourself, letting go of any worldly concerns, and open your heart to God's

presence. Silence creates a space for attentive listening and reflection.

4. Invoke the Presence of God: Begin your reparation prayer by invoking the presence of the Holy Trinity Father, Son, and Holy Spirit. Recognize the divine presence that surrounds you and invite God to be with you as you offer prayers of reparation.

5. Reflect on Your Actions:

Before engaging in reparation prayers, take time to reflect on your own actions and areas where you may have fallen short. This self-examination prepares your heart for repentance and a sincere desire for God's mercy.

6. Use Scriptural References:

Incorporate relevant Scripture passages into your reparation prayers. For instance, meditate on passages that emphasize God's mercy, forgiveness, and the redemptive work of Christ. This adds depth and grounding to your prayers.

7. Express Genuine Contrition:

As you pray, express genuine contrition for your sins and the sins of the world. Acknowledge the impact of sin on your relationship with God and the need for His healing grace.

8. Personalize Your Prayers:

Personalize your reparation prayers by reflecting on specific situations, both personal and global, that require healing and reconciliation. Bring your own intentions and concerns to God in a heartfelt manner.

9. Include Acts of Reparation:

Consider incorporating acts of reparation into your prayers. This may involve making concrete resolutions to avoid specific sins, performing acts of kindness, or participating in charitable activities as a way of making amends.

10. Sustain a Spirit of Gratitude:

Alongside prayers of reparation, express gratitude for God's mercy and the redemptive sacrifice of Jesus. A spirit of thanksgiving reinforces your awareness of God's unmerited love and forgiveness.

11. Be Persistent and Consistent:

Reparation prayers are often part of an ongoing journey. Be persistent in your commitment to prayer and reparation. Consistency allows for a gradual transformation of the heart and a deeper connection with God.

12. Conclude with a Closing Prayer:

Conclude your reparation prayer session with a closing prayer, invoking the blessings of the Holy Trinity, the intercession of the Blessed Virgin Mary, and the guidance of the Holy Spirit. Ask for the grace to live a life reflective of your prayers.

Remember that effective reparation prayers involve an ongoing dialogue with God, a commitment to transformation, and a sincere desire for reconciliation. Approach these prayers with an open heart, trusting in God's mercy and grace.

SECTION FOUR

Prayers Of Contrition

The Prayer of Contrition holds significant importance in the life of a believer, serving as a heartfelt expression of remorse, a plea for forgiveness, and a pathway to spiritual renewal. Here are key reasons highlighting the importance of this prayer:

1. Acknowledgment of Sin:
The Prayer of Contrition begins with a sincere acknowledgment of personal sin. This act of humility is

crucial in recognizing one's shortcomings and the need for divine mercy.

2. Expression of Repentance:
Through this prayer, individuals express genuine repentance for their actions. It serves as a verbal commitment to turning away from sin and striving for a life in alignment with God's will.

3. Seeking God's Mercy:
The prayer is a plea for God's mercy and forgiveness. It acknowledges that God's mercy is the ultimate source of

healing and restoration for a contrite heart.

4. Reconciliation with God:

The Prayer of Contrition is a vital step in the sacrament of reconciliation. It signifies the desire for a restored relationship with God, emphasizing the importance of reconciliation as a fundamental aspect of the Christian journey.

5. A Humble Heart:

This prayer fosters a spirit of humility, recognizing human fallibility and the need for divine grace. It encourages individuals to approach God with sincerity and openness.

6. Inner Transformation:

By uttering words of contrition, individuals invite the transformative power of God's grace into their lives. The prayer becomes a catalyst for inner change, prompting a desire for holiness and virtue.

7. Spiritual Healing:

The act of contrition is a plea for spiritual healing. It acknowledges the wounds caused by sin and entrusts the soul to the Divine Physician for restoration and renewal.

8. Cultivation of Gratitude:

The prayer often includes expressions of gratitude for God's mercy and love. This fosters a sense of thankfulness for the opportunity to seek forgiveness and start anew in the journey of faith.

9. Preparation for Communion:

For Catholics, the Prayer of Contrition is often recited as part of the preparation for receiving the sacrament of Holy Communion. It ensures that one approaches the Eucharist with a purified and repentant heart.

10. Guidance for Daily Living:

Regularly engaging in the Prayer of Contrition serves as a guide for daily living. It encourages self-reflection and prompts individuals to strive for virtuous conduct in their interactions with others.

In essence, the Prayer of Contrition holds profound significance by fostering humility, repentance, and a deepened relationship with God. It encapsulates the core tenets of the Christian faith—acknowledging sin, seeking forgiveness, and embracing God's transformative love and mercy.

Effective prayer for contrition, expressing a sincere plea for God's mercy and forgiveness:

1. Lord, Have Mercy: Please have pity on me, a sinner, Lord Jesus. I sincerely accept my flaws and weaknesses. Please give me the ability to turn from my sin and accept Your unending mercy.

2. Transgression Confession: I come before You, Heavenly Father, to confess my transgressions. I sincerely apologize for the times I disobeyed Your commands. Please pardon me and lead me back to the correct road.

3. Heart Renewal: Gracious God, give me a pure heart. Cleanse me of the stains left by my sins and instill a proper spirit in me again. May Your grace turn me into a loving vessel for You.

4. Contrite Spirit: With a contrite spirit, I approach You, O God. The weight of my transgressions is heavy in my heart. Give me the courage to turn away from sin and toward Your light.

5. Seeking Your Mercy: Please, gracious Lord, grant me Your pardon and mercy. Examine my contrite

heart and, with Your mercy, forgive my transgressions. I put my faith in Your steadfast love.

6. Cleanse My spirit: Please, Holy Spirit, cleanse my spirit. Please wash away the stains of my sin and give me the ability to live a life that pleases God. I pray that Your purifying fire will make me entire and pure.

7. Acknowledgment of Faults: Loving Father, I sincerely accept my shortcomings. I turn to You, asking that You pardon me. Give me the fortitude to walk in Your ways and withstand temptation.

8. Joy Restoration: Please bring back the joy of Your salvation for me, Lord. I turn from my sins and put my trust in Your loving kindness. May Your pardon fill my repentant heart with happiness and tranquility.

9. A Promise to Change: Gracious Redeemer, I promise to turn from my sins and adhere to Your precepts. Give me courage to live virtuously so that I can please You. I am grateful for Your boundless grace and mercy.

May these contrite prayers function as an authentic manifestation of remorse and an intense appeal for God's pity and pardon.

SECTION FIVE

Litany of the Sacred Heart

Lord, please be kind to us.

Christ, please have pity on us.

Lord, please be kind to us.

Christ, pay attention to us.

Christ, please listen to us.

God, the Almighty, please have pity on us.

God the Son, the world's Savior, please have pity on us.

God, send your Holy Spirit to have pity on us.

God, the Holy Trinity, be merciful to us.

Have pity on us, heart of Jesus, Son of the Eternal Father.

Have pity on us, Heart of Jesus, created by the Holy Spirit in the Virgin Mother's womb.

Have pity on us from the heart of Jesus, which is essentially united to the Word of God.

Have pity on us, Heart of Jesus, of immeasurable majesty.

Jesus' heart, the precious sanctuary of God; please extend kindness to us.

Jesus' heart, the Most High's tabernacle; please have pity on us.

Jesus' heart, the heavenly gate and dwelling place of God, please have pity on us.

Jesus's heart, a blazing inferno of charity, please have pity on us.
Have pity on us, Heart of Jesus, dwelling place of justice and love.
Have pity on us from the goodness and love-filled heart of Jesus.
Jesus's heart, the source of all virtues, please have pity on us.
Have pity on us, Heart of Jesus, who is most deserving of all honor.
Have pity on us, Heart of Jesus, King and Center of all hearts.

Have pity on us, Heart of Jesus, in whom are hidden all the treasures of wisdom and understanding.

Have compassion on us, O heart of Jesus, in whom is dwelling the whole of divinity.

Have pity on us from the heart of Jesus, in whom the Father was pleased.

Have pity on us, Heart of Jesus, from whose fullness we have all received.

Jesus' heart, which longs for the eternal highlands, please take pity on us.

Have mercy on us, O patient and most merciful Heart of Jesus.

Heart of Jesus, grant mercy to all who call upon You, and enrich them all.

Jesus' heart, the source of all life and goodness, please have pity on us.

Jesus's heart, please have mercy on us and atone for our sins.

Heart of Jesus, full of scorn, please have pity on us.

Jesus's heart, broken for our transgressions, please have pity on us.

Have pity on us, Heart of Jesus, obedient even to death.

Jesus, who bore a lance wound in his heart, please have pity on us.

Jesus' heart, the source of all comfort, please have pity on us.

Have pity on us, Heart of Jesus, our life and resurrection.

Have pity on us, Heart of Jesus, our peace and reconciliation.

Jesus' heart, the victim of our misdeeds, please have pity on us.

Jesus' heart, please have mercy on us and save those who put their trust in You.

Jesus' heart, the hope for those who pass away in You; please take pity on us.

Jesus' heart, the joy of all the saints, please have pity on us.

Lord, pardon us, through the lamb of God who takes away the sins of the world.

Lord, kindly hear us; we are the Lamb of God who takes away the sins of the world.

Have pity on us, Lamb of God, who takes away the sins of the world.

Jesus, who has a lowly and humble heart, please akin our hearts to Yours.

Let's pray: Almighty and everlasting God, consider the adoration and happiness Your dearest Son bestows upon You in the name of sinners. Please grant them the forgiveness they beg. May their pleas be answered in Your mercy, and may their yearning for justice and salvation be strengthened. Forever and ever, through Your Son, our Lord Jesus Christ, who lives and reigns with You in the unity of the Holy Spirit, one God. Indeed.

SECTION SIX

Sorrowful Mysteries Of The Rosary With A Focus On Reparation

Meditation For The Sorrowful Mysteries Of The Rosary With A Focus On Reparation

First Sorrowful Mystery:
The Agony in the Garden
Prayer:
Lord Jesus, in the garden of Gethsemane, You experienced profound sorrow and agony for the sins of humanity. Grant us the grace

to understand the weight of our transgressions and the courage to seek Your mercy. May our prayers be a humble offering, seeking reparation for the times we have strayed from Your love.

**Second Sorrowful Mystery:
The Scourging at the Pillar**

Prayer:
Dear Jesus, as You endured the brutal scourging, Your flesh torn for our sake, help us recognize the consequences of our sins. May our hearts be moved to genuine contrition, and may our prayers be a

balm for the wounds inflicted by our transgressions. Grant us the strength to turn away from sin and embrace the path of righteousness.

Third Sorrowful Mystery:
The Crowning with Thorns
Prayer:
Lord, as the crown of thorns pressed upon Your sacred head, we acknowledge the mockery and contempt our sins heap upon You. Grant us the humility to recognize the gravity of our actions and the compassion to seek Your forgiveness. May our prayers contribute to the

healing of the wounds caused by our offenses.

**Fourth Sorrowful Mystery:
The Carrying of the Cross**
Prayer:
Jesus, bearing the weight of the cross, You carried the burden of our sins. Teach us to embrace our crosses with patience and humility. May our prayers be an offering of gratitude for Your redemptive sacrifice, and may they contribute to repairing the brokenness we have caused through our transgressions.

Fifth Sorrowful Mystery:

The Crucifixion

Prayer:

Lord Jesus, hanging on the cross, You offered Yourself as a sacrifice for our sins. Help us understand the depth of Your love and the magnitude of Your reparation. May our prayers be a source of comfort to Your wounded heart, and may they lead us to live lives of gratitude and righteousness.

In reparation for our sins, we offer these meditations and prayers through the intercession of the Blessed Virgin Mary. Amen.

SECTION SEVEN

Prayer of Devotion to the Sacred Heart

Devotion to the Sacred Heart of Jesus is a profound expression of love, gratitude, and reparation within the Catholic tradition.

Devotion to the Sacred Heart has deep historical roots, with St. Margaret Mary Alacoque playing a crucial role in popularizing it in the 17th century. The revelations she received from Jesus emphasized His immense love and the call for reparation.

The Sacred Heart is a powerful symbol representing Jesus' divine love, compassion, and sacrifice. Often depicted with flames and a crown of thorns, it signifies the burning love of Christ for humanity despite the wounds inflicted by sin.

A central practice of Sacred Heart devotion is the First Fridays devotion. This involves receiving Holy Communion on the first Friday of nine consecutive months in reparation for sins, fostering a deep communion with the heart of Christ. Many individuals consecrate themselves, their families, and their homes to the Sacred Heart. This act involves a formal commitment to live in accordance with the values of the Sacred Heart, seeking to mirror Christ's love and mercy in daily life. Enthronement of the Sacred Heart in homes is a way of acknowledging Christ's lordship over family life. Families invite Jesus into their homes, seeking His guidance, protection, and blessings.

The Litany of the Sacred Heart is a powerful prayer, enumerating various aspects of Christ's divine attributes. Reciting this litany is a way to express devotion and seek the intercession of the Sacred Heart.

Devotees often engage in a nine-day novena to the Sacred Heart, combining prayers, reflections, and acts of reparation. This focused period of devotion deepens one's connection with the Sacred Heart and emphasizes the transformative power of love and mercy.

Spending a Holy Hour in adoration before the Blessed Sacrament is a cherished practice. During this time, individuals contemplate the love radiating from the Sacred Heart and offer prayers of adoration, thanksgiving, and reparation. Devotion to the Sacred Heart is associated with promises made by Jesus to St. Margaret Mary Alacoque. These include the promise of abundant graces for those devoted to His Sacred Heart and the assurance of final perseverance.

Devotees engage in acts of reparation to console the wounded heart of Jesus, expressing sorrow for sins and seeking to make amends. These acts include prayers, sacrifices, and a commitment to live virtuously.

Devotion to the Sacred Heart is a profound and transformative spiritual practice, inviting believers to deepen their relationship with Christ and to live lives reflective of His boundless love and mercy.

Holy hour of Reparation Prayer, Reflection and meditation to the Sacred Heart of Jesus

In the name of the Father, and of the Son, and of the Holy Spirit. Amen.

PRAYER ONE

O Sacred Heart of Jesus, radiant with love and mercy, I come before you in humble acknowledgment of my sins and the sins of humanity. Your heart, pierced for our offenses, calls us to repentance and reparation. Today, I offer this prayer with a contrite heart, seeking to console and make amends for the wounds inflicted upon your Sacred Heart.

Reflection:

Take a moment to contemplate the image of the Sacred Heart. Visualize the flames of love that emanate from it, burning brightly despite the thorns surrounding it. Consider how your sins may have caused pain to this merciful heart. Reflect on the depth of Christ's love, willing to endure suffering for the sake of your redemption.

Meditation:

Close your eyes and enter into a moment of silence. Imagine standing before the Sacred Heart of Jesus, aware of your imperfections and failings. Picture His gaze of compassion and understanding. In this sacred space, express your sincere sorrow for any offenses, and ask for the grace to truly comprehend the enormity of Christ's love that surpasses all understanding.

PRAYER TWO

Eternal Father, I offer you the wounds of our Lord Jesus Christ, the merits of His Sacred Heart, and the tears of the Blessed Virgin Mary in reparation for my sins and for the conversion of sinners.

Reflection:

Consider the powerful symbolism in offering the wounds of Jesus, the merits of His Sacred Heart, and the tears of the Blessed Virgin Mary. Ponder the concept of reparation, acknowledging that through prayer and acts of contrition, you participate in the redemptive work of Christ.

Meditation:

Visualize your prayers ascending to the heavenly throne as a fragrant offering. Envision the Sacred Heart receiving your intentions with loving acceptance. Allow the grace of reparation to permeate your being, bringing a sense of healing and restoration.

PRAYER THREE

Sacred Heart of Jesus, I trust in your infinite mercy. May the flames of your love purify my heart and lead me to live in accordance with your holy will.

Reflection:

Trust is a key element in reparation. Reflect on your trust in the mercy of the Sacred Heart. Contemplate how this trust can transform your heart, instilling a sense of hope and confidence in God's redeeming love.

Meditation:

In your mind's eye, see the flames of the Sacred Heart purifying your own heart. Feel the warmth and transformative power of His love. Surrender any doubts or fears, allowing the Sacred Heart to become a beacon guiding you on the path of righteousness.

PRAYER FOUR

In the Sacred Heart of Jesus, I place my trust. Amen.

Reflection:

Take a moment to reflect on the sincerity of your prayers and the act of reparation. Consider how this intentional prayer aligns with your desire for spiritual growth and a deeper connection with the Sacred Heart. Acknowledge the transformative power of humility and contrition in fostering a more profound relationship with Christ.

Meditation:

In your quiet moments, meditate on the concept of reparation as a journey of healing and reconciliation. Visualize yourself walking alongside Jesus, allowing His merciful love to envelop you. Let go of any burdens, and trust that the Sacred Heart is a refuge where sins are forgiven, and wounds are healed.

PRAYER FIVE

O Sacred Heart of Jesus, make my heart like unto Thine. Help me to love You more each day and to make reparation for the offenses against Your Most Sacred Heart.

Reflection:

Consider the plea to make your heart like unto the Sacred Heart of Jesus. Reflect on the aspiration to grow in love and virtue, mirroring the qualities of Christ's heart. Ponder how this transformation can impact your relationships, actions, and the way you navigate the challenges of daily life.

Meditation:

Close your eyes and imagine your heart gradually becoming more like the Sacred Heart of Jesus. Picture the virtues of compassion, forgiveness, and selfless love taking root within you. Allow the grace of reparation to shape your character, inspiring acts of kindness, and fostering a genuine desire for holiness.

PRAYER SIX

Sacred Heart of Jesus, I offer myself as a living sacrifice in union with Your Eucharistic Heart. May my life be a continual act of reparation, bringing glory to Your holy name.

Reflection:

Contemplate the profound act of offering yourself as a living sacrifice in union with the Eucharistic Heart of Jesus. Consider how your daily life, struggles, and joys can become a meaningful offering to God. Reflect on the potential for your actions to bring glory to the Sacred Heart.

Meditation:

Envision your life as an offering, laid before the Sacred Heart in the Eucharist. See the transformative power of your sacrifices and challenges becoming a source of grace and reparation. Surrender your life to the Sacred Heart, trusting that through this offering, you participate in the divine plan for redemption.

PRAYER SEVEN

O Sacred Heart of Jesus, may Your love reign in my heart, and may the world come to know and adore Your mercy. Amen.

Closing Prayer:

O Sacred Heart of Jesus, source of all consolation, receive this prayer of reparation as a humble offering. Grant me the grace to live in perpetual gratitude for your boundless love, and may my contrite heart find solace in the mercy that flows from your Sacred Heart. In the name of the Father, and of the Son, and of the Holy Spirit. Amen.

Closing Reflection:

Reflect on the invocation for the reign of the love of the Sacred Heart in your own heart and in the world. Contemplate how, through acts of reparation and a deepened connection with Christ, you can contribute to spreading His mercy and love to those around you. May the Sacred Heart be glorified in your life and bring blessings to the world. Amen.

Closing Meditation:

Take a moment to center yourself in gratitude for the time spent in prayer and reflection. Picture the Sacred Heart of Jesus, radiating love and mercy, surrounding you with a comforting presence. As you prepare to conclude this prayer, carry with you the sense of peace and assurance that comes from seeking reparation in the heart of Christ.

May the grace of the Sacred Heart guide you, and may your journey of reparation be a continuous source of spiritual growth. In the name of the Father, and of the Son, and of the Holy Spirit. Amen.

Final Blessing:
May the Sacred Heart of Jesus bless you abundantly, granting you the

strength to turn away from sin and the grace to live a life of virtue. May His merciful love be a constant source of consolation and may your prayers of reparation contribute to the healing of the wounds inflicted by sin. May the peace of Christ reign in your heart, now and forever. Amen.

SECTION EIGHT

Prayer of Reparation to the Immaculate Heart of Mary

We pray In the name of the Father, and of the Son, and of the Holy Spirit. Amen.

PRAYER ONE

O Immaculate Heart of Mary, adorned with purity and love, I come before you with a contrite spirit, acknowledging my sins and the offenses against your most tender heart. Your immaculate love invites us to seek repentance and reparation. Today, I offer this prayer with a humble heart, seeking to console and make amends for the wounds inflicted upon your Immaculate Heart.

Reflection:

Pause and reflect on the beauty and purity of the Immaculate Heart of Mary. Contemplate the profound love and grace that emanate from her heart, even in the face of our human failings. Consider how your own actions may have caused distress to this Mother who loves you unconditionally.

Meditation:

In the quiet of your heart, imagine standing before the Immaculate Heart of Mary. Picture her gaze of maternal compassion, understanding the struggles and imperfections of your life. Offer to her the burdens of your sins and shortcomings, trusting in her intercession for forgiveness and healing.

PRAYER TWO

O Immaculate Heart of Mary, in union with the Sacred Heart of Jesus, I offer you my contrite heart. Receive my prayers of reparation and may they console your tender heart wounded by the sins of humanity.

Reflection:
Consider the profound union between the Immaculate Heart of Mary and the Sacred Heart of Jesus. Reflect on how your prayers of reparation can be a source of comfort to the heart of the Mother of God. Acknowledge the interconnectedness of these two hearts in the divine plan of redemption.

Meditation:
Envision the Immaculate Heart of Mary receiving your prayers with

maternal love. Imagine her presenting these prayers to the Sacred Heart of Jesus, joining them with His redemptive sacrifice. Allow a sense of unity and intercession to permeate your soul as you entrust your petitions to Mary's immaculate hands.

PRAYER THREE

Most Blessed Mother, I seek your guidance and protection. May your Immaculate Heart be a refuge for my contrite spirit, leading me closer to your Son, Jesus.

Reflection:

Contemplate the desire for guidance and protection from the Immaculate Heart of Mary. Reflect on how seeking refuge in her heart can bring solace and lead you closer to Jesus. Acknowledge the maternal care and intercession that Mary offers to those who turn to her with contrite hearts.

Meditation:

Close your eyes and imagine being enveloped by the protective mantle of the Immaculate Heart. Sense the peace and warmth emanating from her heart, guiding you on the path of virtue and holiness. Allow her maternal presence to instill in you a renewed sense of trust and confidence in God's mercy.

PRAYER FOUR

Immaculate Heart of Mary, Queen of Heaven, I consecrate myself to your maternal care. Help me to live a life of purity, humility, and love in reparation for my sins and those of the world.

Reflection:

Reflect on the act of consecration to the Immaculate Heart of Mary. Consider the commitment to live a life aligned with virtues of purity, humility, and love. Acknowledge the transformative power of consecration in fostering spiritual growth and reparation.

Meditation:

Visualize yourself consecrating your life to the Immaculate Heart of Mary. Picture her accepting your offering with a loving smile, guiding and nurturing you as her child. Feel the grace of consecration shaping your intentions and actions, leading you on a journey of spiritual renewal.

PRAYER FIVE

Immaculate Heart of Mary, may your purity and love inspire me to be a channel of grace and mercy in the world. In your gentle hands, I place my contrite heart. Amen.

Closing Reflection:
Reflect on the inspiration drawn from the purity and love of the Immaculate Heart of Mary. Consider how, by entrusting your heart to her, you become a vessel of grace and mercy in the world. Carry this inspiration with you, knowing that the Immaculate Heart is a source of strength and guidance. Amen.

In the name of the Father, and of the Son, and of the Holy Spirit. Amen.

Closing Meditation:

Take a moment to breathe deeply and absorb the peace that comes from offering prayers of reparation to the Immaculate Heart of Mary. Imagine her gentle presence surrounding you, guiding you towards a life of greater purity and love. Feel the grace of this moment, knowing that your contrite heart is received with maternal tenderness.

May the Immaculate Heart of Mary, our loving Mother, intercede for us before the throne of God. May her purity and love be a guiding light on our journey of faith. In the name of the Father, and of the Son, and of the Holy Spirit. Amen.

Final Blessing:

May the Immaculate Heart of Mary, full of grace and compassion, bless you abundantly. May her intercession bring you closer to the heart of her Son, Jesus. May your prayers of reparation contribute to the healing of wounds and the renewal of hearts. May you walk in the light of her love, now and forever. Amen.

Personal Reflection:

As you conclude this prayer, take a moment to reflect personally on the emotions and thoughts that surfaced during this time of meditation. Consider any insights or feelings that arose as you communed with the Immaculate Heart of Mary. Allow these reflections to deepen your awareness of the need for repentance, healing, and a closer relationship with the Blessed Mother.

Resolution for Action:
In the spirit of reparation and consecration, consider a practical resolution. It could be a specific act of kindness, a commitment to

avoiding certain behaviors, or an intention to deepen your prayer life. Write down this resolution and keep it as a tangible reminder of your desire for spiritual growth and alignment with the Immaculate Heart of Mary.

Immaculate Heart of Mary, as I conclude this prayer, I carry with me the grace of this moment. Strengthen my resolve to live in accordance with your purity and love. Guide me, dear Mother, and intercede for me before your Son. Amen.

Closing Blessing:

May the Immaculate Heart of Mary, our compassionate Mother, continue to watch over you and intercede on your behalf. May her purity and love inspire your daily life, and may your journey of reparation be guided by her maternal care. May the blessings of the Immaculate Heart be with you always. In the name of the Father, and of the Son, and of the Holy Spirit. Amen.

SECTION NINE

Additional prayers of reparation to the Sacred Heart of Jesus

1. Prayer of Reparation for Personal Sins:

Most Sacred Heart of Jesus, I offer You my sincere contrition for the times I have strayed from Your commandments. In Your boundless mercy, forgive my sins, heal the wounds caused by my transgressions, and grant me the grace to turn away from sin and embrace Your divine love. Amen.

2. Prayer of Reparation for the Sins of the World:

O Sacred Heart of Jesus, we humbly come before You, seeking reparation for the sins of the world. In Your infinite compassion, look upon humanity with mercy. May our prayers and acts of reparation contribute to the healing of the wounds inflicted by sin and bring about conversion and renewal. Amen.

3. Act of Consecration and Reparation:

Sacred Heart of Jesus, I consecrate myself to Your divine love and offer reparation for the offenses committed against Your Sacred Heart. In union with the Immaculate Heart of Mary, I dedicate my life to serving You and spreading the message of Your mercy. Amen.

4. Prayer for the Conversion of Sinners:

Most Merciful Heart of Jesus, we lift up to You those who have turned away from Your love. In Your infinite compassion, draw them back to the path of righteousness. May our prayers and acts of reparation be a source of grace for their conversion and redemption. Amen.

5. Prayer of Reparation in Times of Persecution:

O Sacred Heart of Jesus, in times of persecution and hostility, we turn to You for strength and courage. We offer reparation for the offenses against Your Holy Name. Grant fortitude to Your Church, and may our prayers alleviate the suffering endured by Your faithful. Amen.

6. Prayer for Healing and Restoration:

Loving Heart of Jesus, we seek Your healing touch for the brokenness within Your Church and the world. In reparation for division and discord, pour out Your grace of unity and reconciliation. May Your Sacred Heart be a source of healing and restoration for all. Amen.

7. Prayer for Those Who Desecrate the Sacred:

Sacred Heart of Jesus, we offer prayers of reparation for those who desecrate Your holy name and disrespect the sacred. In Your mercy, touch their hearts with the grace of conversion. May our acts of reparation contribute to the restoration of reverence for Your divine presence. Amen.

8. Prayer for the Unborn and the Culture of Life:

Precious Heart of Jesus, in reparation for the sin of abortion and the culture of death, we offer our prayers. Heal the wounds caused by this grave offense against life. May Your love inspire a culture of life, and may our reparation hasten the day when all life is cherished and protected. Amen.

9. Prayer for Victims of Injustice:

Compassionate Heart of Jesus, we lift up to You the victims of injustice and oppression. In reparation for the sins that perpetuate suffering, grant strength to the afflicted and justice to the oppressors. May our prayers contribute to a world where Your love prevails, and justice and mercy reign. Amen.

10. Prayer for Final Perseverance:

Sacred Heart of Jesus, in reparation for the times we have faltered, we implore Your grace for final perseverance. May our hearts remain steadfast in Your love, and may our lives be a continual offering of reparation, leading us to the eternal joy of Your divine presence. Amen.

May these prayers of reparation to the Sacred Heart of Jesus be a source of solace, healing, and grace for you and for all humanity. Amen.

SECTION TEN

Additional reparation prayers to the Immaculate Heart of Mary

1. Prayer of Contrition and Reparation:

Immaculate Heart of Mary, Queen of Heaven, I come before you with a contrite heart, acknowledging my sins and the sins of the world. I offer these prayers in reparation, seeking your intercession for forgiveness and healing. May your Immaculate Heart be a refuge for the repentant and a source of grace for our wounded world. Amen.

2. Act of Reparation for Offenses Against Mary:

Most Pure Heart of Mary, we offer this act of reparation for the offenses committed against you. In sorrow for the blasphemies and ingratitude, we seek your mercy. Help us, dear Mother, to console your Immaculate Heart and to live in accordance with your virtues. Amen.

3. Prayer for the Conversion of Sinners:

Immaculate Heart of Mary, in reparation for the sins that wound your tender heart, we lift up all sinners to your maternal care. Intercede for their conversion and guide them to the mercy of your Son. May our prayers be a source of consolation for your Immaculate Heart. Amen.

4. Offering of Reparation for Abuses and Injustices:

Immaculate Heart of Mary, we offer prayers of reparation for the abuses and injustices that grieve your maternal heart. May our acts of penance and prayers contribute to the healing of those wounded by sin. May your intercession bring about justice and mercy in our world. Amen.

5. Prayer for Victims of Persecution:

Immaculate Heart of Mary, in reparation for the persecutions against your children, we seek your protection and intercession. Console those who suffer for their faith and inspire us to stand in solidarity with them. May our prayers alleviate their pain and bring about an end to persecution. Amen.

6. Prayer for Families in Need of Healing:

Immaculate Heart of Mary, we offer prayers of reparation for families in need of healing. Intercede for those torn apart by discord and strife. May your gentle presence bring reconciliation and peace to every home. Amen.

7. Act of Consecration and Reparation:

Immaculate Heart of Mary, I consecrate myself to your loving care and offer acts of reparation for the offenses committed against you. Help me to live in accordance with the purity and love that radiate from your Immaculate Heart. Amen.

8. Prayer for an End to Abortion:

Immaculate Heart of Mary, in reparation for the sin of abortion, we offer prayers and acts of penance. Help us to foster a culture of life and to protect the unborn. May your motherly intercession bring about a conversion of hearts and an end to this grave offense. Amen.

9. Prayer for the Conversion of Hearts:

Immaculate Heart of Mary, in reparation for the hardness of hearts, we implore your intercession. Soften the hearts of those who have turned away from God and lead them to the fount of mercy. May our prayers contribute to a world transformed by love and conversion. Amen.

10. Prayer for the Triumph of Your Immaculate Heart:

Immaculate Heart of Mary, we offer these prayers in reparation and with hope for the triumph of your heart. May your Immaculate Heart prevail, bringing about the fulfillment of the promises at Fatima and ushering in an era of peace. Amen.

May these prayers of reparation to the Immaculate Heart of Mary be a source of grace, healing, and consolation. Amen.

CONCLUSION

Engaging in reparation prayers, whether directed to the Sacred Heart of Jesus or the Immaculate Heart of Mary, is a profound spiritual practice that calls for sincerity, humility, and a genuine desire for reconciliation with God. Throughout this prayerful journey, the emphasis lies not only on acknowledging and seeking forgiveness for personal sins but also on offering prayers and acts of reparation for the offenses committed against the Sacred and Immaculate Hearts.

It is crucial to create a sacred space for reflection, invoking the presence of the Holy Trinity and immersing yourself in moments of silence. The incorporation of Scriptural references and the personalization of your prayers deepen the connection with the divine, allowing for a more meaningful dialogue with God.

Expressing genuine contrition, reflecting on your actions, and including acts of reparation in your prayers are essential components of this spiritual practice. The act of contrition fosters humility, while self-reflection promotes an awareness of the need for God's mercy and healing. Acts of reparation extend beyond words, becoming tangible expressions of repentance and love.

Let your journey of reparation prayers be sustained by a spirit of gratitude, acknowledging the unmerited love and forgiveness extended by God through the redemptive sacrifice of Jesus. Persistence and consistency in prayer foster a gradual transformation of the heart, leading to a deeper connection with God and a more authentic Christian life.

In your concluding moments of prayer, seek the blessings of the Holy Trinity, the intercession of the Blessed Virgin Mary, and the guidance of the Holy Spirit. Ask for the grace to live a life reflective of the prayers offered, cultivating virtues of love, mercy, and humility.

May the reparation prayers you offer be a source of solace, healing, and grace for yourself and for the world. May the Sacred and Immaculate Hearts be pleased with your sincere efforts, and may you continue to walk in the light of God's mercy, now and always. Amen!

Made in United States
Troutdale, OR
04/15/2024